Elissy's World
A Turkish Delight

Written by
Claudia and Annelise Myrie

Illustrated by
Vladimir Cebu LLB

Copyright © 2023 by Claudia and Annelise Myrie

All rights reserved.

No part of this book may be reproduced or used in any manner whatsoever without written permission of the copyright owner except for the use of brief quotations embodied in critical article or book review.

DEDICATION

To Elissy,

You're such an incredible child!
You can do anything you set your mind to.
Never stop reaching for your dreams,
because even if you stumble along the way,
we will be there to pick you up and cheer you on.

Love, Mum and Dad

To all the amazing children, yes, you reading!

I'm so proud of you. Keep questioning, learning, and discovering.
It's a great big world out there—go explore!

Love, Elissy

From the moment Elissy set foot on Turkish soil, she could sense something was wrong. All around her, people in long, white-sleeved shirts and flowing white skirts with what looked like thimble hats on their heads scurried along the pavement.

"Where is it?" someone yelled.

"How can it just be gone?" another asked.

"Is it stolen?" came the response.

"Elissy looked at her mom and whispered, "It seems like they lost something! We need to investigate!"

With a confident stride, Elissy tapped on the shoulder of a pale-faced man and asked, "Pardon me, Sir. What is it that you have lost?"

"The Mevlana Whirling Dervishes Festival is about to begin and no one can find the Turkish Delight. Without our traditional sweet treat, spectators can't come and watch the show because they won't have anything to eat!" the man replied.

"Turkish Delight?" Elissy frowned as she watched the man walk away.

"Turkish Delight is a cube-shaped sweet that smells a lot like roses. It melts in your mouth and has been made traditionally in Turkey since the 18th century! What a sad sight to see these people searching for the pink-coloured candy!" Elissy's mom said.

Happy to have her big book of letters safely packed away in her backpack, along with her Explorer Badge, Elissy took her mom's hand while taking the first step of her new adventure.

"We need to search far and wide," Elissy said thoughtfully. "Those letters can hide anywhere and if we don't find them all, there won't be enough sweets to go around!"

Elissy rubbed her tummy as she thought of the candy disappearing without being eaten.

"Look!" Elissy pointed towards one yellow and one red letter beneath a bush by the side of the road. "It's the letters E and A!"

"These letters could belong to the fact that Turkey is in between two continents called Europe and Asia," Elissy's mom suggested.

"Yes!" Elissy shouted. "We found two letters belonging to a fact!"

Carefully, Elissy picked up the two letters, placed them in her backpack and wrote down the fact on a notepad.

"Come on, we need to pick up the pace, those Turkish Delights are waiting to be found!" Elissy pulled on her mom's hand as she led the way.

While making their way into a park, Elissy looked around at the hundreds of trees lining the grassy field.

"Could a letter be hiding in one of these trees?" Elissy asked her mom.

"We need to search in every nook and cranny if we want to find all the facts needed to complete this quest!" Elissy's mom said as she helped her strong-willed child climb on a large tree.

Within minutes, Elissy sat on the highest branch while scanning the park.

"There!" she pointed. "I see something! In the fountain in the middle of the park!"

Elissy scrambled down the tree and ran up to the fountain spraying water not far from the tree she climbed into.

And sure enough, soaking wet and covered in moss, a red letter **S** lay under the surface of the murky water. Elissy picked it up and shook it, trying to get the droplets and slimy moss to fall off the letter.

"What fact does the letter S belong to?" Elissy looked at her mom.

"Well, it might belong to the fact that Santa Claus comes from Turkey and not the North Pole, as we might have all believed. Born in Turkey, a man named Nicholas, who we later renamed Santa Claus, used to drop bags of coins down the chimney for poor families to find on Christmas morning," Elissy's mom confirmed.

"Amazing!" Elissy said as she wrote down the fact and placed the letter in her backpack.

After all this searching, are you not thirsty?" Elissy's mom asked.

Elissy swallowed and nodded.

"Let's grab a cup of tea at the street vendor standing at the entrance of the park. Once we feel refreshed, we can continue our quest to find the missing letters and their facts," Elissy's mom suggested.

After paying for two tulip-shaped cups of tea, Elissy's mom handed her a refreshment. Elissy sipped at the warm sweetness and sniffed at the calming aroma surrounding her cup. As she took another sip, she nearly spat out her tea!

At the bottom of her cup, a small white letter T stared back at her!

Gently, she picked it out of her cup and held it up into the air for her mom to see, "I found another letter!"

"Hmmm…" Elissy's mom thought for a moment. "The letter T can belong to the fact that Turkish people love drinking tea. Over 96% of citizens living in Turkey drink at least one cup of tea a day!"

Elissy took the last sip of her tea, placed the letter in her backpack and wrote down the fact.

"Oh no!" Elissy whined as they walked down the street. "My shoe broke!"

Elissy picked her broken white sandal up and showed it to her mom. "I can't search for letters all across Turkey with a broken shoe on my foot!"

"You're right," Elissy's mom agreed. "We need to get you some new shoes before we continue our adventure."

At a large mall, Elissy and her mom found a pair of sparkling gold and silver shoes. After Elissy's mom paid for the sandals, Elissy sat down to put them on.

Something wasn't right. They were the right size but something kept scratching her left foot's big toe!

Peering into the shoe, Elissy was surprised to find a gold-covered letter M hiding in the lining of the shoe.

"Mom, look what I found! I found the letter **M**!" Elissy exclaimed as she pointed to the tiny letter in her shoe. "Does the letter M belong to a fact about Turkey?"

"Let me see..." Elissy's mom scratched her head. "The letter M can belong to the fact that Turkey has one of the oldest malls in the world. In fact, we are standing in it right now! This mall was built all the way back in the year 1455!"

Fascinated with the fact, Elissy placed the letter M in her backpack and wrote the fact down on her notepad.

As they walked through the mall, Elissy's tummy rumbled.

"I sure wish we can find all the facts in time! It will be a very sad thing to see all the Turkish Delight disappear!" Elissy said as she listened to her hungry tummy asking for something to eat.

"What about I get us some hazelnuts as a snack?" Elissy's mom asked as she stopped at a stall to buy some fresh nuts.

Thanking her mom, Elissy took a plastic bag filled with hazelnuts and started munching on the healthy snack. Biting down hard, the crunchy sound of her teeth grinding the nuts made Elissy laugh.

"Ouch!" Elissy yelled as she bit down on something unusually hard.

Looking down at her hand while expecting to see a nut, Elissy gasped as she saw brown coloured letter **H** with bite marks on it.

"Look!" Elissy showed her mom. "I nearly ate the letter H!"

Inspecting the letter, Elissy's mom said, "The letter H belongs to the fact that Turkey is the world's largest producer of hazelnuts. The weather here is perfect for growing these nuts!"

As Elissy munched on another nut, she wrote the fact down and added the letter to the rest of the alphabet in her backpack.

"We have been walking for hours and have not found another letter!" Elissy said as they searched the city streets.

Elissy's mom wiped beads of sweat from her head and looked at the map she was holding in her hand, "This city sure is large! It will take weeks to get to the other side!"

"We don't have that much time!" Elissy replied urgently as she frantically looked from side to side. "We only have one more fact to find. There is no way we can give up now."

Elissy's mom lifted her hand into the air, waving at a taxi driver, "We would have to make our way back to the location of the festival. We may not have found all the facts but we tried our very best! I am not sure how much longer I will be able to walk!"

Nodding while feeling a little defeated, Elissy jumped into the back seat of the taxi and waited for her mother to get in.

"Greetings!" the taxi driver said. "As a gift, I am giving all my passengers a keyring to remind them of their journey in Turkey!"

Elissy accepted the gift and turned to her mom in surprise. In her hand, attached to a metal ring, a shiny letter I danced.

"The letter I!" Elissy squealed. "It has to belong to the last fact!"

"We are in the largest city in Turkey named Istanbul…" Elissy's mom said thoughtfully.

"That's it! We found the last fact!" Elissy exclaimed excitedly as she placed the gift in her bag while scribbling down the last fact.

As soon as the taxi driver stopped in front of the festival location, Elissy jumped out. In front of the door, the same woman stood, looking into the crowd lining the street. She seemed worried.

"Oh, dear child!" she called as she saw Elissy running toward her. "Were you able to find all the facts?"

Elissy nodded as she emptied her backpack on the large table in front of the building. Then she placed her notepad with facts alongside it.

"Such a brave explorer you are!" the woman beamed as she pointed toward the table with empty silver plates.

Before Elissy's eyes, a mountain of sugared cubes fell from the air. Everyone looked up and saw the Turkish Delight rain down onto the table, covering all the plates with sweet treats.

The crowd, relieved and clapping, thanked Elissy and her mom for saving the festival.

"Come on, join us!" the woman said as she opened the doors.

Elissy closed her eyes as she put a Turkish Delight in her mouth. It tasted delicious!

Music started playing as a group of people dressed in white shirts, white skirts and thimble-shaped hats made their way to the centre of the building.

Feeling like she had been transported to a fairytale land, she watched as the group danced. Their skirts flowed in the breeze and their hands, clasped above their heads made it look like they were thanking the world for its gifts. The entire audience was enchanted by the sight as the group moved in circles with their heads tilted to the side.

As the festival came to an end, Elissy had made up her mind. Turkey, with its breathtaking culture, great attention to detail and ability to make anyone feel welcome definitely deserved a top spot on her Explorer List!

"Dear girl," a woman said as she walked by, "Would you be so kind to help us search for the missing Delight?"

"Why, yes!" Elissy replied with eyes open wide, "I'd love to help!"

"Such a kind child you are! All you have to do is find letters of the alphabet belonging to 6 different facts about Turkey. Once you find these facts, you need to bring them to the festival's front door. Only then will the Turkish Delight reappear and the festival will be able to start; but beware, for dangers are lurking around the corner…" the woman warned.

"I won't let you down!" Elissy reassured the frightened lady.
Before the woman disappeared into the crowd, she whispered in Elissy's ear, "Hurry, for there is not much time! With every passing second, another cube of Turkish Delight will disappear forever!"